Queenstown
Stories Behind the Scenery

Queenstown
Stories Behind the Scenery

Photographs by Mike Hollman
Text by Sue Hall

Hodder Moa

National Library of New Zealand Cataloguing-in-Publication Data
Hall, Sue, 1951–
Queenstown : stories behind the scenery / Sue Hall & Mike Hollman.
ISBN 978-1-86971-163-4
1. Queenstown (N.Z.)—Description and travel. 2. Queenstown (N.Z.)—
Pictorial works. I. Hollman, Mike. II. Title.
919.39500222—dc 22

A Hodder Moa Book
Published in 2009 by Hachette New Zealand Ltd
4 Whetu Place, Mairangi Bay
Auckland, New Zealand

Designed and produced by Hachette New Zealand Ltd
Printed by 1010 Printing International Ltd., China

Front cover: Queenstown from Lake Wakatipu
Back cover: Moss Vale Falls, Mt Aspiring National Park; snow mobile on Coronet Peak;
TSS *Earnslaw* on Lake Wakatipu

Contents

Queenstown–Lakes district

An introduction

Residents on the shores of lakes Wakatipu, Wanaka and Hawea must wake up each morning, open the curtains and blink again in awe at the splendour of their surroundings. Shadows ripple across crystal-clear lakes, verdant valleys run into forested slopes and majestic mountain ridges fill every backdrop. The scenery in New Zealand's Queenstown–Lakes district is some of the most spectacular our planet can offer.

The intensely alpine countryside reveals an astonishing variety of landforms, having been folded, faulted and glaciated over aeons. Vistas from the high country are broad — often as far as the eye can see — and they bring wonder and humility to anyone who visits.

This is a grand and beautiful landscape with crisp, clear light. Artists and photographers, casual and professional, become absorbed in catching the changing reflections and shadows on lakes, rolling hills and sharp ridges, excited by so many juxtaposed contrasts.

Not only do lights and moods change during the day, four distinct seasons in the district make the colours and

Lake Wakatipu

stimuli of the landscape change dramatically throughout the year. In autumn the towns and lake edges are ablaze with yellows, golds and vivid reds. Winter snow transforms the mountains into white-capped wonderlands, sharp against clear blue skies. In spring, green landscapes flower into vibrant bursts of colour and, as the long hot days of summer approach, the high-country tussocks turn gold.

For early Maori, in search of pounamu (greenstone/jade) and the flightless moa, and nineteenth-century gold miners and farmers, in search of fortune and lifestyle, the landscape provided inspiration and aspiration. Today, for residents and visitors this region has an irresistible attraction.

Queenstown is a resort area of unrivalled scenic diversity where 'anything is possible'. If hurtling along — with wind rushing past your ears, your lips pulled into a grimace of joy — is your kind of pleasure, then Queenstown, the 'adventure capital of New Zealand', is the place for you. Here you will find mountain sports, water sports and airborne sports of all descriptions. If your approach is more measured — walking, tramping, touring and absorbing beauty — Queenstown is also the place for you. Tourists, outdoor-adventure seekers, film makers, photographers, golfers and wine buffs — not to mention Queen Elizabeth II and a US president — have all been drawn to this spectacular alpine wonderland.

So popular is the lakes district that the average daily population of 35,000 can swell to peaks of 75,000 and more when the Winter Festival and fresh snow weave their magic spell.

Landscape in formation

The dramatic landscape of the Queenstown–Lakes district was born over aeons. Slipping continental plates, moving mountains and gouging glaciers have all made their mark.

Because New Zealand sits astride two continental tectonic plates — the Pacific and Australian — the country is in constant movement, performing an aeons-long geological pirouette. The boundary between the plates runs through New Zealand in the Marlborough region in the South Island, cuts across to the west coast then continues south along the Alpine Fault and runs back out to sea near Milford Sound, 80 kilometres (50 miles) or so west of Queenstown.

On this Alpine Fault the Southern Alps have formed. The two continental plates are colliding at a glancing angle, causing the bedrock to buckle and squeeze upwards. Some mountains have formed with cracked and jagged ridges through folding and buckling. Others, by contrast, have long straight sides where blocks have been pushed up along major faults. It's these contrasts that make the Alps and the lake districts so beautiful.

Skiing at Coronet Peak

9

Although the Southern Alps are among the fastest-rising mountains in the world, there's no reason to get excited about seeing mountains in action! These things take time. They are rising at a rate of one to two metres (three to seven feet) per century — hardly visible. But, to make the landscape more complicated and interesting, the land is also

the ice ages and large amounts of snow fell on the mountains (forerunners to our Southern Alps), accumulated and steadily hardened into ice. The ice followed gravity and chiselled its way downwards and into the valleys in the form of huge glaciers.

As they clawed their way down, these marauding conveyor-belt monsters took rock

The Remarkables

being wrenched apart. Along the Alpine Fault the bedrock to the west is moving north-east at two to three metres (seven to 10 feet) per century relative to the bedrock on the east.

The mountains are rising. So why don't they rise till they topple? Because alpine ridges are also sculpted, eroded and eaten away by glacial, frost, water and wind action. Two and a half million years ago, the earth plunged into

with them and dumped massive ridges, called moraines, at their leading edges and along their flanks. As temperatures fluctuated, glaciers retreated and advanced, gouging and dumping, gouging and dumping. Glacial debris was flushed down further by rivers, filling river valleys with thick gravel.

The ice-sculpted landforms that are seen in the lakes district today are the product of

Lake Hayes

advances and retreats within the last 250,000 years and the most extensive moraines date back only 18,000 years. Glacial activity now is confined mainly to higher mountain regions, but there is evidence everywhere of earlier, more widespread activity. Rock faces show giant scratch marks where ice scraped its way past. U-shaped valleys hang suspended above wide valleys, evidence of smaller tributary glaciers that used to run into larger flows. Mountainous ridges of moraine remain, some blocking valleys which have then filled with water to form lakes.

According to Maori legend most of the lakes in the area were formed by chief Te Rakaihautu who, using his mighty ko (digging stick), hollowed out the inland lake beds and formed the mountains from the spoil.

Sailing on Lake Wakatipu

Lake Wakatipu

Easily identifiable on the map because of its lightning-bolt shape, Lake Wakatipu is New Zealand's third largest lake and the second largest in the South Island. It is a deep, long and narrow canyon, 84 kilometres (52 miles) long and, at its widest point, 5 kilometres (3 miles) wide, left in the wake of a huge ice-age glacier. Mountains run straight into the lake.

Not only is it grand and of stunning beauty, Lake Wakatipu has a curious side to its nature. High in alpine country, its surface is 309 metres (1014 feet) above sea level but, with a depth of 377 metres (1237 feet), its deepest point is 68 metres (223 feet) below sea level. It also has a curious heart beat, rising and falling by about 10 centimetres (four inches)

TSS *Earnslaw* on Lake Wakatipu

every 25 minutes or so. Science describes this oscillation as a seiche, caused by wind or atmospheric-pressure variation. At Bobs Cove, the best place to observe it, the variation is about 12 centimetres (almost five inches) every five minutes.

Maori legend, on the other hand, describes it as the heart beat of Matau, a giant who was burnt to death in his sleep because he abducted a chief's daughter. He lay curled on his side, his body burning a hole in the rock and the snow and ice melting to form the lake waters. His head lay where the town of Glenorchy is now, his knees at Queenstown and his feet at Kingston. His heart still pumps, causing the rise and fall of the lake. It is impossible to destroy a giant's heart.

History

Maori first came to Lake Wakatipu in search of moa, a large cumbersome flightless bird that was relatively easy to hunt as a food supply. They also came for pounamu, the highly valued greenstone or jade used for tools, weapons, ceremonial carving and personal adornments. An area north of Lake Wakatipu is one of six of the country's main sources of pounamu.

The ancient trails used by Maori took the shortest and less difficult routes. As a result, many are now the sites of modern roads.

Queenstown's first European settler, William Gilbert Rees, established the first farm in the area in 1860, burning beech forest to make way for pasture exactly where the town of Queenstown is now. His brother-in-law, Nicholas von Tunzelmann, the son of a Russian aristocrat, settled the west side of the lake near the Greenstone River.

Although Rees made his land productive it was not all rural bliss for him. In 1862 gold was discovered in the Arrow River and Rees suddenly found himself at the centre of a gold rush. Not only that, he found himself the only source of food for hungry miners. His world was turned upside down. But he rose to the occasion, his dominant personality giving him unquestioned authority in the region. With a flock of sheep and the first boat of any size (the *Undine*) on Lake Wakatipu he brought flour and other supplies from the south end of the lake. Rees was able, for a few vital weeks, to prevent starvation among miners. He is now revered as the founding father of Queenstown.

Rees knew he lived somewhere very special. It was he who brought the area around Lake Wakatipu to the attention of the editor of the *Otago Witness* in 1859. The editor prophetically wrote:

> The information indicates the country around the Wakatipu is in all probability a gold bearing district . . . should the precious metal be discovered the 65 miles of inland water carriage would be such an immense advantage that in all probability the country would be extensively wrought.
>
> But apart from any consideration of wealth to be derived from the mineral resources of the country, the existence of

Lake Wakatipu

such lakes as are to be found in Otago will, we have no doubt, at some future date, cause this part of New Zealand to be extensively visited for the mere purpose of viewing the grandeur of the same.

Even then, there was realisation that Queenstown would eventually be the major tourism hub it is today.

The year 1900 farewelled gold fever around the lake, the population subsided to about 200 and runholders more peacefully farmed the lakeshores and hill country. Queenstown was visited for supplies and its beauty, not for its gold.

Flora and fauna

Right: Kowhai flower
Below: Shag, Lake Wakatipu

Before the arrival of the gold miners and pastoralists, the Wakatipu Basin was a shrubland dominated by species such as manuka and the thorny matagouri. The cover of native bush and mountain beech forest in the shady gullies was home to many species of birds. Tui, bellbird, huia and kokako song rang around the lake. On the hillsides, tussock herbfields, with sharp-pointed speargrasses and native flowers, blanketed the slopes.

Moa had become extinct through hunting by Maori prior to Europeans' arrival, but fire, pasture and invasive plant species and animals introduced by European miners and farmers altered the ecological balance in the area forever. Bush was cut or burnt to make way for grass, sheep and cattle. Many bird species such as the huia, deprived of their natural habitat, became extinct and others, such as the kokako (a wattlebird), gradually retreated into the deep untouched forests of Fiordland — where its enigma lives on. The South Island kokako was declared officially extinct in 2007, but persistent rumours of its haunting evocative call still have conservationists

trekking deep into the bush to find it.

Rabbits were introduced into Southland in 1867 and, within about 15 years, had bred to plague proportions, and spread throughout the South Island. The rabbits, in competition with sheep, were winning the nibble war. Farmers were forced to take drastic measures, some going bankrupt and leaving their farms. In the 1880s stoats, weasels and ferrets were introduced to control the rabbit numbers, but, tragically, native birds were easier prey.

Today, the hillsides and towns of the Wakatipu Basin are dotted with exotic trees and shrubs. Plants such as blackberries and briar rose were introduced by early settlers as a good source of vitamin C, and were useful as hedge plants. Tending to spread out of control, they covered large areas. Even now they wage a constant battle with farmers and conservationists.

Many forces are at work in providing the stunning variety and beauty of the Wakatipu environment. Native trees and shrubs and splendid golden-foliaged exotics live side by side. Native songbirds are heard in the forest and bushlands, and in town gardens introduced and native birds sing alongside each other. The relatively unmodified braided river areas at the west end of the lake provide habitat for rarer native and migrant birds including wrybill, black-billed gulls, black-fronted terns, banded dotterels and oystercatchers. Birds such as shags and ducks dive and dabble in and around the cool deep waters of the lake and, much to anglers' delight, brown trout feed around the edges. Deeper in the lake, rainbow trout and salmon take their chances against ensnaring hooks.

The three main Lake Wakatipu islands — Matau (Pig Island), Wawahi-Waka (Pigeon Island) and Tree Island — are free of rodents, stoats and weasels, and are therefore sanctuaries providing important opportunities for native species' recovery.

Glenorchy

Forty-five minutes north-west of Queenstown, at the headwaters of Lake Wakatipu lies the small town of Glenorchy, familiarly called 'the Wakatip'. Peaceful and remote from the nightlights and social bustle of Queenstown, this tiny historic town is the hub of a tranquil eco-wonderland.

The Glenorchy Valley, with calm waters, lively birdlife, golden tussock, ancient native beech forest and braided rivers, is the perfect natural gateway to the splendour of the Mt Aspiring National Park. The park, formed in 1964, almost doubled in size by 1990 and was declared part of Te Wahipounamu — the Southwest New Zealand World Heritage Area. This designation recognises its beauty

Glenorchy Library

and significance to global landscape conservation.

Trampers leave from Glenorchy to explore some of the finest hiking tracks in the world: the Rees and Dart Tracks, the Greenstone and Caples Tracks or the world-renowned Routeburn Track. Rising into alpine altitudes, these old pathways wander through an astonishing array of lakeside, forest, subalpine and alpine vegetation — a constantly changing feast for the eyes — from massive beech trees and podocarps to lichens, mosses, fungi, native orchids and alpine flowers.

The Dart Valley is a stronghold of the yellowhead or mohua, an endangered songbird. Often the mohua is the main birdsong heard in the valley. Confiding New Zealand robins hop close to trampers, finding insects in the disturbed leaf litter.

Other less-known and equally beautiful tracks are also accessed here, some by horseback, some by foot or mountain bike, some tracing the histories of the scheelite (tungsten ore) miners who set up the town of Glenorchy. Kayaking, jetboating, heli-skiing, skydiving, fishing or canyoning can also be on the itinerary, providing varied ways of experiencing the grand untamed wilderness.

Miners working scheelite deposits in the Dart and Rees river valleys in the 1860s built the town of Glenorchy, intent on developing an income and lifestyle. Land nearby was burnt for pasture. However, by the turn of the century, scheelite mining was becoming uneconomic and settlement failed to expand. The quaint historic town that remains today still proudly preserves many of the original miners' buildings.

Much of the former pastureland around the town is now covered in regenerating shrubland and young forest with a high plant diversity. Most of the land below the road has not been farmed or burned for around 30 years and eventually (in about 150 years), if undisturbed, will become red beech forest, adding to the languid tranquillity of this lake's end.

Fungi on the Routeburn Valley forest floor

The head of Lake Wakatipu, looking towards Glenorchy

Queenstown

Queenstown, an adventure resort of world renown, is sited on the banks of Lake Wakatipu — at the knee of the sleeping giant, Matau. It has established itself as a boutique alpine venue offering an incredible range of activities, no matter what the season. Dubbed 'the adventure capital of New Zealand', the sophisticated cosmopolitan town buzzes with skiers in the snowy season, offers luxury and affordable accommodation to travellers all year round and is a major centre from which to source adventure activities in the lakes district.

The astonishing variety of activities is a reflection of the range of landscape — both tamed and wilderness — and whatever is embarked on, the backdrop is always stunning. A sample of what's on offer includes scenic tours and flights, guided walks, tramping, bungy-jumping, jetboating, rafting, skiing and snowboarding, heli-skiing, skydiving, paragliding, hang gliding, horse riding, kayaking, canyoning, safari tours by four-wheel drive or snowmobile, hunting, fishing, golf, mountain biking and ballooning.

Queenstown from Lake Wakatipu

The town is also a magnet for wine buffs wanting to enjoy boutique dining and explore the 82 wineries registered in the Otago region.

Queenstown township is an invigorating, upmarket alpine resort boasting more and more European-style architecture and everything within walking distance. The compact centre has excellent shopping for outdoor clothing, sports gear and woollen goods, and shops stay open until 10 pm. There is something for everybody.

From dusk to dawn Queenstown rarely sleeps. Sophisticated wine bars provide good food, live music and top DJs. With over 160 licensed cafés and bars, the socialite is spoilt for choice any night of the week, any day of the year, either in a garden bar serving local wines and locally brewed beer or for après-ski in front of a roaring log fire.

Winter Festival

The Winter Festival is an annual 10-day celebration of winter in the mountains and the ultimate winter party. Based around Queenstown and at the Coronet Peak ski-field, in June or July, the action-packed days of fun and festivities on and off the slopes have been a huge success for almost 30 years and attract visitors from all over New Zealand, Australia and around the globe. Parties, races and exhibitions, a mardi gras in the street, comedy shows, music concerts, teddy bears' picnic, arts and crafts, night skiing, fireworks, a float parade, ice hockey, snow sculpture, jazz nights, celebrity ski races, the Festival Ball and a night-time hot-air balloon glow can all be part of the fun.

Snow machines at Coronet Peak

A view over the town

Since it opened in 1968, well over 11 million people have ridden the Skyline Gondola into the hills behind Queenstown to look out over the town and Lake Wakatipu. The view is almost too beautiful to believe: the majesty of The Remarkables (the rugged range of snow-capped mountains to the south-east), the peninsulas of ancient moraine (the Kelvin Heights golf course and the Queenstown Gardens) that appear to ooze into the lake at the entrance to Frankton Arm, and long clear waters disappearing into the distance, reflecting mountains, snow and clouds. Justifiably, this is one of the most-photographed views in the lakes district.

Waterfront, Queenstown

Queenstown Botanical Gardens

Queenstown possesses one of the country's most scenic botanical gardens. On an adjacent peninsula of ancient moraine at the foot of The Remarkables and jutting out into Lake Wakatipu, colourful flowerbeds are set amid beautifully tended lawns and huge exotic trees, planted long ago. The rose garden boasts over 20 varieties.

Birdsong from the bellbird or tui is intermingled with the thwack of racquets hitting tennis balls and lawn bowls clicking against each other in the Domain. From the Queenstown side visitors can see views of the town, as well as the TSS *Earnslaw* steaming out on a sightseeing trip. From the far end of the peninsula there are views down the lake and, on the return down the far side, views of Frankton.

Queenstown Botanical Gardens

Shotover Jet

Queenstown Botanical Gardens

TSS *Earnslaw*

A much-loved Queenstown survivor is the graceful vintage steamship TSS *Earnslaw* which leaves from downtown Queenstown Wharf on scenic tours of Lake Wakatipu. Affectionately known as the 'Lady of the Lake', the 51-metre (167-feet) twin-screw steamer, operating since 1912, is the last of a long line of coal-burning steamers working on Lake Wakatipu from as early as 1863.

Visitors at the turn of the twentieth century — when tourism began in earnest — were not very complimentary about the standard of comfort offered by the privately owned steamers on the lake, designed mainly for carrying cargo for lakeside runholders. Old photos show the foredecks of such ships as a seething mass of woolly sheep. The majestic Lake Wakatipu was,

at the time, being likened to the alpine setting of Switzerland's famous Lake Lucerne — so there was a reputation to uphold.

The government decided to step in. It bought out the steamer company, immediately rescheduled the runs to coincide with the famous Kingston Flyer train services from Gore to Kingston at the south end of the lake, and commissioned the building of TSS *Earnslaw*. The carrying capacity of their new bigger, better steamer was 1035 passengers and 100 tons of cargo (or 1500 sheep, 200 bales of wool or 70 head of cattle). Crew comprised 11. She carried goods, shepherds and their dogs, horses, farmers, tourists, shearers, wool and livestock, motor cars, and even buses en route on tourist trips.

The 'Lady of the Lake' has been transporting goods to remote settlements and conveying passengers on beautiful Lake Wakatipu for over 97 years. Today it also makes regular

TSS *Earnslaw*

Deer Park Heights

scenic cruises on the lake and takes passengers 13 kilometres (eight miles) across the lake to Walter Peak High Country Farm.

Walter Peak Station

Walter Peak Station was one of the most historic of high-country runs in the country. In its heyday it spread across 69,000 hectares (170,500 acres) of rugged mountain farmland, carried 40,000 sheep and had 50 fulltime employees. The station took its name from nearby Walter Peak mountain, named for Queenstown's founder William Rees, in recognition of his son Walter Cecil.

It is still a working high-country farm today but comprises 26,000 hectares (64,000 acres), runs 1800 sheep and 1000 cattle. Subdivision has wrought its toll on the original large station.

Walter Peak High Country Farm resort, on 155 hectares (380 acres), provides walking tours through the farmyard. Visitors can feed sheep and get up close to deer and Scottish Highland cattle and walk to the woolshed to watch sheepdogs in action, sheep being shorn and wool being spun. The beautiful old Colonel's Homestead is now a grand restaurant and bar for all-day dining.

Eichardt's Hotel

Several historic buildings remain within burgeoning Queenstown. The stories of the grand Eichardt's Private Hotel reach back to

its inception as a canvas-covered tavern called the Queen's Arms, built by William Rees (the founder of Queenstown) on his farmland. Raw and basic, the Queen's Arms was one of 17 licensed and unlicensed hotels in the area during the height of the gold rush. It catered for thirsty gold miners and travelling merchants — and its reputation was not the best!

A series of partnerships with others saw Rees gradually change the nature of the hotel towards a more family-oriented business with accommodation. In 1867, he sold it outright to his partner Albert Eichardt and C.C. Boyes for £150.

Twenty years of ownership by the

government-owned Tourist Hotel Corporation from 1957 to 1977 did little to improve the hotel, which still was only big enough to accommodate 38 people. Fortunately for the building's place in history, the Corporation's plans to build a new five-storey hotel on the site failed to get government approval. During this period maintenance was minimal, occupancy rates fell and the building lost its status, declining from hotel to motor inn and finally to Eichardt's Tavern. It was a return to private enterprise that brought Eichardt's back to life and allowed the grand old building to survive constant threats of demolition.

Lake views from on high

Off the road to Kingston on the east side of Lake Wakatipu a road meanders up through Deer Park Heights (a private farm park) to the top of Kelvin Heights. This is an ideal spot for walkers, mountain bikers and tour guests to look out over incomparable scenery, while also getting up close to exotic 'open plains' animals such as miniature horses, Shetland ponies, pigs, donkeys, alpaca, llamas, bison, yaks, long-haired Highland cattle, goats, sheep, mountain thar and, of course, several varieties of deer.

So dramatic is the scenery that the site has been chosen as the location for several films. For six weeks in the autumn of 2001 the elevated grasslands and the rugged Remarkables became the backdrop of Middle-earth in Peter Jackson's *The Lord of the Rings: The Two Towers*. The 1986 Walt Disney children's movie *The Rescue*, released on video, was also filmed here. The movie had an overall budget of NZ$18 million, and the Korean Prison — built for the movie at a cost of NZ$1 million and used over 20 days of filming involving many local people — still stands near the top of the heights.

More spectacular aerial views over Lake Wakatipu open up from the lookout points on the road up to the Remarkables Skifield. In snowy conditions this alpine road needs to be approached with great care.

Walter Peak High Country Farm

The Skippers Road, looking toward Skippers Canyon

Skippers Canyon

No self-respecting adventure seeker misses a day trip from Queenstown to Skippers Canyon. The narrow, unsealed road that snakes its way through the spectacular Skippers Canyon hugs the cliffs and 'levitates' over the roaring Shotover River. Vertical drops to the river, negotiating slips on the road and cautiously edging past other vehicles are all part of the ever-memorable, 17-kilometre (11-mile) Skippers Road experience. It makes the visitor appreciate anew the isolation experienced by settlers and miners in this remote place.

Most rental companies warn their clients not to travel on this road, so many people choose to join a tour — so they can concentrate on the scenery, rather than the driving! And wonderful scenery it is. Dramatic schist bluffs and rock tors stand like sculptures in the tussock-draped landscape. The road commands views of the Richardson Mountains to the west and the Harris Mountains to the east.

In November 1862 two hopelessly broke men arrived on William Rees' property looking for work. Thomas Arthur and Harry Redfern were duly employed as shearers but, during some of their down time, the two wandered off to a place now called Arthurs Point on the Shotover and found more gold than they had ever dreamt of. Sheep shearing was suddenly no longer an option. Working as fulltime miners, they took out £4000 worth of gold in two months (an absolute fortune in 1862). Within six months the Shotover canyon was swarming with 4000 miners, all hoping to earn £4000 each!

The route in was dangerous and difficult. Miners often had to be lowered down precipices by rope. In winter the trail through the snow was marked by red poles set in the ground and connected by wire, but despite the hardships miners kept coming as the area proved to be very fruitful.

Once the alluvial gold started to run out, the miners turned to sluicing, dredging and quartz mining. The need for a road to the Skippers settlement was crucial when heavier mining equipment was required.

Built between 1883 and 1890 in four sections, the Skippers Road was considered an engineering feat in its day. Nowadays, increased road usage has meant that much of the original engineering has been altered or eroded away. Miles of stonewalling, built up from locally quarried schist, topped off with capping stones on the outer road edge, once curved their way through Skippers Canyon. Today these stone memorials are becoming scarce.

Now, tour companies with buses and four-wheel-drives lure visitors here, not just for the scenery or history, but for a range of exhilarating adventure sports from rafting or jetboating the Shotover, to leaping off the historic Skippers Bridge or the pipeline bungy, to mountain biking part of the original 1860s pack track.

One of the world's most famous jetboat operations skims the waters of the Shotover River daily, and that's thanks to a New Zealand inventor, Sir William Hamilton (OBE), who, in 1953, built the world's first jetboat. Using waterjet propulsion, and avoiding the need for low-slung propellers, jetboats can travel up shallow, fast-flowing water. They are ideal for the gravelly rapids of the lakes district's glacial rivers and, much to the exhilaration of tourists, can spin in 360-degree turns and manoeuvre very close to rocky edges.

Coronet Peak

Off the Skippers Canyon Road an equally exciting road winds up to Coronet Peak. Here is another of the lakes district's wonder playgrounds of snow and ice, drawing thousands of skiers, boarders and après-skiers from all round the globe to participate in social and competition skiing. In what better place could you be on top of the world? Verbal competition rages annually as to which of the district's skifields affords the best snow, best activities, best amenities and best views . . . but, as long as there's snow, people keep flocking in.

Sunset over Coronet Peak

Kingston

After the busy social life and the lure to conquer the elements near Queenstown, there is no quieter and more relaxed place than Kingston. Forty-eight kilometres (30 miles) south of Queenstown and on the southernmost tip of Lake Wakatipu, the town of Kingston — named after a country town in Ireland — was once a major link for the southern goldfields and runholders.

In the 1860s some 5000 people passed through the Kingston Wharf onto steam boats carrying them to the Wakatipu goldfields. Transport to the area was transformed when the Kingston Flyer steam-train passenger service opened. Operated between the Main South Line at Gore and the Kingston Station, from 1878 through to the mid 1950s it provided a more secure passageway to Queenstown and the surrounding stations. Tourist numbers swelled and, accordingly, the number of lake steamers increased.

The most notable of the steamships was TSS *Earnslaw*, which still plies the lake waters. Built in parts in Dunedin

The Kingston Flyer

by the government in 1911, and the parts then railed to Kingston, the twin-screw steamer was erected on the lakeshore. A commemorative plaque marks the site of the *Earnslaw* slipway.

Kingston's premier attraction is now the restored vintage steam train, 'The Kingston Flyer'. The two AB Pacific Class steam locomotives and seven steam-heated wooden vintage carriages have a combined history that spans over 125 years.

Nowadays, The Flyer makes excursions between Kingston and Fairlight twice daily from October to April. At the stations there are recreational amenities, walking tracks, fishing, a nine-hole golf course and a bowling green.

The geology of Kingston

The rail track, wharf and town of Kingston are all built atop an ancient moraine. As the Dart Glacier retreated around 10,000 years ago, during the last ice age, it left a huge glacial valley behind it. The highest terminal moraine spanned the valley (where Kingston is today) and shut off the flow to the Mataura River. Lake Wakatipu formed behind it. Unable to empty into the Mataura because of the vast heaps of moraine gravel, the lake was forced to carve out a new passage to the sea, further north, via the Kawarau Gorge and the Clutha River.

Arrowtown

Avenues of vibrantly coloured trees and carpets of burnt orange and gold are always an invitation to frolic during the autumn months at Arrowtown and nearby Lake Hayes. The golden leaves, reflected in lake waters or lining town streets, are the legacy of European farmers and early gold miners. In the late nineteenth century these folk slaved away to exploit and tame the alluvial gravels and rocky green-forested and tussocked wilderness around the Arrow River.

The waters here run clean and clear and the lake waters teem with birdlife, trout and salmon.

Only 20 minutes from Queenstown, Arrowtown is a charming and picturesque town filled with rich heritage. The past is

Arrowtown in winter

Autumn in Arrowtown

preserved in miners' cottages, historic wooden buildings, and nineteenth-century-style shops, still standing as they did during the gold rush. It is a living historic town. The main avenue, Buckingham Street, famous for its mature sycamores and oaks, and other trees splendid in autumn, provides an array of shopping opportunities. An original grocer's store still plies its trade, as does a gold shop and jade-carving shop. There are also several quality clothing shops, craft shops, souvenir shops, wine shops, cafés and restaurants.

The Stone Cottage, built around 1870 for a mining agent, has since been used by a dressmaker, bankers and lawyers. Today it houses tearooms. The Arrowtown Jail, built in 1876, replaced the old log jail that had accommodated the unruly from 1863. The Stables was built in the 1860s and is a good example of local rock construction with thick walls and small windows.

Even the Lakes District Museum is housed partly in an original 1875 Bank of New Zealand building, a fitting environment for its vibrant presentation of the town's extensive history.

To the north of Arrowtown, on the banks of Bush Creek, is the partially restored and well-interpreted Arrowtown Chinese Settlement, built by Chinese miners from 1869. Ah Lum's Store and outhouse (now preserved through registration as a historic place) operated until 1972. Long after the gold-rush days were over the store continued to serve the increasingly infirm elderly Chinese who resided in the settlement until their deaths.

At the height of the gold rush, the population — including miners camped beside the river — grew to over 7000. The bustling town became the hub of a larger community including the new quartz-mining towns of Macetown, Skippers and Bullendale (now ghost towns). After the initial rush passed, it developed from a mining town into a permanent community, which included several hotels, a bank, post office, jail, school and hospital.

Nowadays, farming and viticulture are major income earners. Arrowtown is a well-established centre of production for many award-winning wines, and vineyard tours and wine trails around the area are always on offer.

Tourism activities include horse treks, hot-air balloon rides and bush walks, and lottery fans can even test their mettle gold-panning the local rivers. If the quiet life beckons, upmarket resorts and local accommodation provide access to fishing or simply the opportunity to relax and absorb the picturesque local scenery.

The Chinese Settlement

When gold was found on the South Island's West Coast region in 1865, the population of Arrowtown, and Otago generally, plummeted. Concerned for the development of the district,

the Otago Provincial Council invited Chinese miners from Victoria, Australia to come to the goldfields. Within two years there were 1200 Chinese in Otago and this total quadrupled in the 1870s.

Often victims of discrimination, the Chinese lived on the fringes of European settlements in isolated gullies close to their mining claims. They were also a valuable source of cheap labour. In the Arrowtown region, Chinese men earned five shillings a day carrying out street repairs for the borough or working for builders. It seems their reputation as workers was excellent but their remuneration was considerably less than the £3 a week paid for European labour. The Presbyterian Church in Arrowtown was erected with a great deal of Chinese labour.

In 1869 the local newspaper recorded:

> The Chinese element is beginning to be largely predominant here and a stranger entering the town during the usual dinner hour at noon, or at 'knocking-off time' in the evening, would almost imagine that he was in a sort of miniature Hong Kong.

Local distrust persisted and anti-Chinese agitation and petitions were launched in 1871, but, bravely, the local paper championed the Chinese in pleasant terms.

> I consider the Chinese population are a great benefit to the district. They exhibit an amount of energy and perseverance most creditable to themselves and benefit to the community of which

Arrowtown

they form a portion. Their business transactions as a rule appear to be upright and straightforward, while they are most orderly and sober in their general habits.

European miners were fearful of the Chinese, initially because of competition for claims, but in the main the Chinese were content to work over claims already abandoned by Europeans. Nevertheless, there was continuing prejudice because the Chinese were perceived as an economic threat, especially during the depression of the 1880s. To dissuade further immigration a poll tax was introduced, but by this time (1881) mining was on the decline. Those Chinese who remained drifted off to market gardening or commerce, forming the basis of the present Chinese community.

By 1885 the settlement at Bush Creek had grown to consist of about 10 huts, a large social hall and at least two stores. There was also an extensive garden area. A range of construction techniques was used for the buildings, including mud brick, mortared slabs of schist, wood, corrugated iron and canvas. Some buildings were thatched while others were roofed with corrugated iron. An old photograph of 'Tin Pan', a late resident in the settlement, is annotated with a claim that he lived beneath a roof of four flattened kerosene tins.

It is worth noting that the names used by authorities to describe the Chinese in gold-mining Arrowtown almost invariably bear little or no resemblance to the person's true name or to their literal translation. The local Chinese used their true names when among themselves, but, regrettably, the true names have been lost.

Historic cottages, Arrowtown

Local geology

From the Crown Terrace viewpoint there's a great opportunity to see evidence of the massive glacial action that carved out the Wakatipu Basin. Looking round the lake it is easy to notice the difference between the rounded forms of the hills and the much higher, jagged peaks such as at Walter and Cecil Peaks. The rounded hills were once covered by glaciers and were smoothed off by the force of the ice, but were strong enough to resist the glacier's push through the landscape. The sharp peaks, however, have always been above the height of even the largest, oldest glaciers.

The rock in the surrounding hillsides, and under the town, is schist — a colourful layered rock patterned with stripes and myriad shiny mica specks. It is the rock most common in the Arrowtown area and was used in construction by early settlers. It was also the basis of the gold and quartz mining in the district.

In a process called metamorphosis, layers of 250-million-year-old volcanic rock and sedimentary material were combined under pressures of 4–5000 times normal atmospheric pressure and temperatures up to 400°C (752°F). Schist was the result, interspersed with layers of quartz, seams of gold, and copper.

It was the gravel eroded from these rock layers by glaciers, frost action and water that provided opportunity for miners to pan for alluvial gold in the local rivers. Once that source was exhausted the miners turned to sluicing the river banks with jets of water in the hope that higher alluvial gravels would reveal their 'load'. Dredges explored the gravels below river level. By the 1870s advancements in mining methods allowed them to crush the gold-bearing quartz in the quartz reefs.

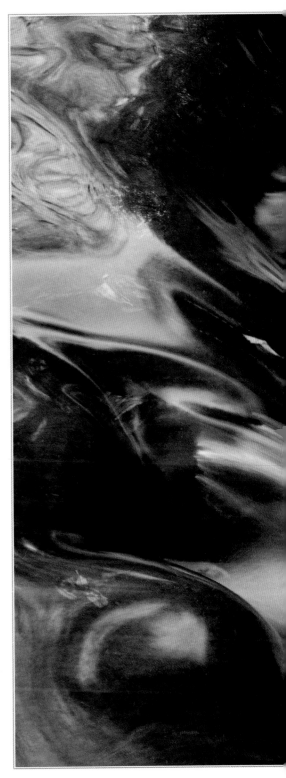

A country stream in Arrowtown

Lake Hayes

Kawarau River

The Kawarau River is the only outlet for the mighty Lake Wakatipu. The lake waters ease through ancient moraine into Frankton Arm and then flow generally eastwards, picking up volume and speed for about 60 kilometres (37 miles) until they reach Lake Dunstan near Cromwell. Beyond there, they feed into the mighty Clutha River system.

Between Frankton and Lake Dunstan, the river waters are added to by the Shotover River and the Arrow River. The combined flow then takes a tortuous course through the steep Kawarau Gorge. Further south, the Nevis River and Roaring Meg add volume and intensity before the river meets Lake Dunstan.

The road that winds through the gorge was not always as easy to negotiate as it is today. The precipitous bluffs on the southern side of the main road at the entrance to the Kawarau Gorge from Queenstown have proved a major obstacle to traffic into the Wakatipu Basin ever since William Rees and Nicholas von Tunzelmann first

Shotover River, a feeder to the Kawarau River

settled in the area. Original foot tracks from the south wound round bluffs and headlands and followed much the same line as the old Maori greenstone trail — used by Maori when passing through the area in search of pounamu — descending into Arrowtown via 'Tobins Track'.

In 1866, a new road, more suitable for horse and cart, was built along the south side to replace the rather hazardous northern track. Picks, shovels, wheelbarrows, gunpowder poured into drill holes, blood, sweat and endurance paved the way through schist cliffs and promontories. The Morven Ferry punt took travellers across the Kawarau River — but only when the weather and river levels allowed it. In a huge step of progress, in 1880, a bridge was constructed to bypass the unreliable punt.

The river still meanders and roars, drawing thousands of sightseers and adventurers. Some 10–15,000 people raft, kayak, board or sledge the river each year. Others choose to jetboat it or jump over, or into, it by bungy. Others choose to just look — or walk the many scenic and historic tracks surrounding it.

Bungy-jumping over the Kawarau River

The Battling Betty Bridge was built over the Kawarau River in the 1960s to replace the one built in 1880. With the construction of State Highway 6 the bridge was unused and fell into disrepair. It was only the audacity, courage, bravado and ingenuity of two 'madmen' that brought it to life again.

Inspired by men from Vanuatu who (in a manhood ritual that developed over hundreds of years) threw themselves from towers with vines attached to their feet, New Zealanders A.J. Hackett and Henry van Asch set about proving that they could do the same with modern materials and from higher launching points.

Their first successful jump was from a ski gondola in the Tignes skifield in France. Their second (unlicensed and controversial) jump, in June 1987, was from the Eiffel Tower — to the astonishment of nearby gendarmes. The jump set the world press abuzz and put the men's efforts onto the world stage.

A year later, in 1988, it took another leap of faith to set up the world's first commercial bungy-jump venture at the Kawarau Bridge near Queenstown — a leap that projected AJ Hackett's Bungy New Zealand into national and global success.

From the bridge, 20 minutes east of Queenstown, brave and adventurous visitors can bungy 43 metres (141 feet) on an elasticised cord to the river below. Their panicking or delighted screams follow them down and then up as the bungy cord pings them skywards again. The choices are: to leap either upside

down, forwards, backwards or in a harness with a friend; or to either bob above the water, touch the water or get a dunking.

The not-so-brave can watch and ooh and aah from the safety of large wooden decks built into the rock face over the river.

For adrenalin junkies there is another hair-raising bungy ride some 10 kilometres (6 miles) eastward. The Nevis Highwire Bungy plunges a breathless 134 metres (440 feet) towards the rugged Nevis River, and with 8.5 seconds of freefall this bungy is not for the faint-hearted!

To add to the thrills, the recently opened Nevis Arc — at the end of a 70-metre-long (230-feet) walkway — is the highest swing in the world, spanning 120 metres (394 feet) and reaching speeds up to 125 kilometres per hour (78 miles/hr). Where will AJ Hackett Bungy New Zealand ever draw the line?

Even as a small boy, apparently, AJ never knew where to draw the line when it came to adventure and ingenuity. On the local television programme *This Is Your Life*, he revealed that, at an early age, he attached a top deck to his trolley: a box set on four dowels above the driver's seat. AJ perched himself in the top deck, his friend steered the trolley fast downhill and around a corner. The top deck parted company with the trolley and AJ was launched on one of his earliest trajectories.

Bungy-jumping over the Kawarau River

Gibbston Valley

Queenstown and Central Otago is the fastest-growing wine region in New Zealand. It is also New Zealand's highest.

The Gibbston Valley, 15 kilometres (9 miles) from Arrowtown, has been developing as a strong wine region since the 1980s and is proving itself to be an ideal *terroir* for continental-style wines. Its semi-continental climate, with immense extremes in seasonal and daily temperatures, combined with gravelly well-drained loam soils with heavy deposits of mica and schist, give wines the intensity and vibrancy of mountain air. The conditions — found in some of the greatest vineyard areas of the world, most notably the inland cool climates of Central Europe,

Gibbston Valley winery

Chard Farm winery

Burgundy, Alsace, Champagne and South Germany — are ideal for the production of Pinot Noir and Pinot Gris.

Renowned for Pinot Noir, the Queenstown and Central Otago wine region has won more gold medals for this variety than any other New Zealand region. Chardonnay, Sauvignon Blanc and Pinot Gris varietals are also held in very high regard. Gibbston Valley now has nearly 300 hectares (740 acres) planted in grapes, making it about one-tenth of the total Central Otago vineyard area.

The valley is known to have cooler conditions than most. Because it lies in the rain shadow of the mountains it generally experiences warm and dry summers, low rainfall during the growing season, and cool nights. Consequently, a longer growing season pushes back the harvest dates. To the joy of the winemaker, this slow ripening can enhance the build-up of colour and flavour.

Equally, of course, unseasonable frosts can bring heartbreak. But nobody wants to dwell on those!

The winemakers of the region are hardy, innovative and business savvy. Having broken in their vineyards from merino sheep country or orchard lands, they have developed world-class wine venues with wines of matching quality. The diversity of alluring cellar doors,

restaurants and conference rooms in a variety of building styles — from the simplicity of an 1893 church, to modern buildings with award-winning architecture — is testament to their ingenuity and passion.

At Peregrine Winery they 'utilise modern plant with traditional practice'… and modern plant it is! The much-photographed winery building, whose roof soars and dips in harmony with the land, earned its architects a winning place in the prestigious London-based ar+d emerging architecture awards. The jury described the winery as 'an elegant blade of light [that] contrasts with the rugged and sublime natural landscape. The age-old process of making wine has been radically reinterpreted for our time.'

Other innovators experiment with time-tested techniques in the search for ideal methods in a new *terroir*. The barrel cellar at Chard Farm uses the old-world technique of sitting the barrels on bare earth pits that have been filled with gravel. This: 'lets the cellar breathe, but more importantly keeps the humidity high, thereby preventing a lot of wine evaporation (aka "the angels' share") and therefore loss of wine. This is particularly important in the low natural humidity climate.'

In the Gibbston Valley, one of the world's most picturesque wine regions, the wine lover is spoilt for choice. There are few greater pleasures than to sip a little bottled sunshine under a vivid blue sky in clean mountain air.

Wine, cheese and produce to please

Another epicurean delight is the Gibbston Harvest Festival. First held in March 2006 at the initiative of a small group of Gibbston-based wineries, it is modelled on European festivals and follows in the footsteps of harvest celebrations held in the 1990s at the district's first winery, Gibbston Valley Wines. The number of wine and food producers participating is growing each year.

Because the valley is surrounded by mountains the boundaries are very clearly defined, which has given the growers a unique identity. Each year a different winery is selected to provide the festival venue and the emphasis is on a casual family picnic atmosphere. One hundred per cent of ticket sales revenue goes to local charities.

Popular among visitors and locals are the locally hand-crafted cheeses from Gibbston Valley Cheesery. The cheese styles, all made using traditional methods, have a natural synergy with the local wines.

The specialty is sheep's milk cheese; the milk being 'harvested' from East Friesian sheep in Southland, milked from late October to late February each year. Fresh styles of cheese such as feta and white mould cheese are made over the summer. Others, such as Balfour — their signature cheese — are hard-pressed and matured to develop a sweet nutty flavour.

Friesian and Jersey cow's milk is also used to produce a variety of dairy cheeses such as Brie, Havarti style, double creams and cheddar.

Wanaka district

The winding road east of Arrowtown, which crosses the Crown Range to Wanaka, looks like a short cut on the map. It is only 62 kilometres (38 miles) long but takes almost the same time to traverse as the 117-kilometre (73-mile) State Highway 6 route through Cromwell — about one-and-a-half hours. It is the highest main road in the country, rising to 1121 metres (3678 feet), with magnificent views at various points on the way, to Arrowtown, the snaking Kawarau River and across to The Remarkables range. Frankton, Queenstown and part of Lake Wakatipu come into view at the summit.

The vista northwards on the steadily downward drive through the Cardrona Valley is possibly one of the best ways to view the splendid isolation of lakes Wanaka and Hawea — a hidden alpine paradise. The Southern Alps stretch ahead into the snowy or misty distance, with the two lakes, like shining oases, within their lee.

A third of the way down, a winding and challenging drive upwards (especially in icy conditions) on the road to the Cardrona skifield opens out incomparable panoramas.

The Cardrona Hotel (est. 1863)

(Arguably, though, the views from the Treble Cone skifield road on the western side of Lake Wanaka might compare.) Cardrona is yet another major piste that lures local and international skiers. Equally popular is Snow Farm — a second skifield off the Cardrona Road — which specialises in cross-country skiing and Nordic sports. A range of 18 or so cross-country skiing trails run near curious car-trial tracks that have been installed for testing prototype vehicles in a range of conditions.

Tailings from old gold-mining operations are still visible further down the Cardrona Valley road. From 1870, thirsty miners slaked their thirst at the Cardrona Hotel … and locals, trampers, skiers and tourists have done the same ever since. The genuine historic building, rooted to its original foundation only a step away from the road's edge, combined with modern beers and great coffee, make this a congenial and popular destination. Other historic buildings from the tiny settlement still stand nearby.

One story often heard at the hotel tells of James Paterson, a long-serving publican who took over the hotel in 1926. He served warm beer from bottles closed with corks, didn't serve women and rationed his patrons — one glass for those travelling over the Crown Range and two for those heading to Wanaka. He could join the traffic police these days on reputation alone!

Lakes Wanaka and Hawea

Excavated by massive glaciers, lakes Wanaka and Hawea lie side by side, only a narrow neck of land separating them where the glaciers used to join. Both lakes are fed by snow and ice melt from the 2000-metre (6560-feet) mountains that surround them. Lake Wanaka empties directly into the Clutha River, New Zealand's second

Lake Wanaka

longest but fastest-flowing river. The waters of Lake Hawea empty into the Hawea River and eventually add to the volume of the Clutha.

Lake Wanaka is ringed by pebbly beaches. Summer sun sparkles on the water and as the autumn days get crisper the banks are a blaze of heart-warming colours. No wonder this is a playground for boaties, kayakers, paragliders and swimmers — beautiful, calm and accessible waters in an alpine Arcadia.

In winter it is more the mountains that call, the three local international skifields (Treble Cone, Cardrona and Snow Farm) opening as soon as there is enough snow.

The township of Wanaka is equally welcoming, with the considerable attraction being that it is still essentially a country village, not as developed as Queenstown. The relaxed social scene — either summer al fresco or winter log-fire après-ski — however, is also attracting many wealthy residents and more and more large expensive homes are creeping in around the township.

The Wanaka–Mt Aspiring Road

Walking tracks and trails wander the shores of the lakes and in the surrounding foothills. For challenging all-day walks, a zigzagging track off the Wanaka–Mt Aspiring Road, round the southern side of Lake Wanaka, leads up to the 240-metre (787-feet) summit of Mt Roy, and a circular track winds its way up Mt Iron, both affording spectacular views over the surrounding peaks, lakes, valleys and rivers. The circular track on Mt Iron clearly shows the effects of glaciation on the bedrock. The mountain is oriented in the direction of the glacier's flow and the upstream side is smoothed and rounded while the downstream side is rough and jagged.

Further along this road is the winding mountain road to Treble Cone skifield, another alpine piste where ski blades carve a path through the silence of the mountain tops and people gather for après-ski bonhomie.

Lake Wanaka

Moss Vale Falls, Mt Aspiring National Park

The Matukituki Valley — pathway to Mt Aspiring

For a remote nature stroll without vertical challenge, a walk along the end part of the Matukituki Valley road is a gentle excursion typical of the incomparable wilderness experience possible in these parts. Meandering alongside a wide gravelled and braided river with the sounds of rapid water and birdsong in the air and lofty mountains on all sides, it is the ideal 'walk to lunchtime'. For anything further up the valley, however, full tramping regalia and equipment are a necessity as this is another track into the alpine Mt Aspiring National Park and a route to Mt Aspiring itself. In its upper reaches the river reaches fever pitch, providing the ideal venue for guided canyoning.

The Matukituki Valley has been home to runholders since the 1860s. A succession of hardy farmers and their wives have battled the elements in this valley, the early ones setting up house on the western side of the river (near the firewood supply). With the need to take their flocks to Wanaka for shearing, losses of stock in the river were high. Three cursed crossings of the river had to be negotiated between the homestead and the road end. In 1885 Ewen Cameron lost 80 per cent of his flock in a storm. In 1899 the river claimed the life of runholder Hugh Macpherson and, during the First World War, Duncan Macpherson's wife drowned in the river when her gig overturned. The homestead area is signposted today as Cameron Flat...and the lack of a bridge there can only leave you pondering.

Wanaka township

Rock climbing and abseiling, indoors or outdoors; jetboating; archery; minigolf; quad bike, go-kart and monster-truck rides; and scenic flights into Mt Aspiring National Park that can link up with guided walks and jetboating adventures — all can be sourced in the quaint little town of Wanaka, with its cafés and restaurants looking out over the lake edge.

At Cinema Paradiso the small-town feeling prevails. Patrons sit on old living-room-type

entrenched in Wanaka township at the town's quirkiest attraction. Stuart Landsborough's Puzzling World started as a three-dimensional maze but has now burgeoned into a full-out assault on your powers of reason and sense of space. A series of eccentric buildings and illusion rooms challenge your sensory systems.

Wanaka's Puzzling World

sofas, or even the front seats of Morris Minor cars. Homemade ice cream and cookies are served at intermission and a meal and glass of wine can also be ordered, but the priority is to get there early to claim the best seat!

Equally well-known in the Wanaka/ Aspiring region is the Landsborough family name — there is even a river named after them. But the name has been forever

Warbirds Over Wanaka

Every year Wanaka is centre stage for an extravaganza of aerial action by warbirds, classic planes and modern jet aircraft. The town accommodation is booked out months in advance as aeroplane fanatics and those who just love a dramatic display converge on the town. It is as much the theatrical alpine stage that draws them as the extraordinary variety of machines. Fourteen thousand attended the inaugural show in 1988. The number has swelled to 80,000.

And not all the action is in the air. The airshow also provides a complete entertainment package for the whole family with a feast of aviation attractions on the ground.

Lake Hawea and the road to Haast

Even if you're not planning to travel up the South Island's beautiful West Coast, it is worth making a day trip from Wanaka into the Haast Pass/Tiora-patea to experience, even from your car, some of the best alpine and lake scenery in the country. The trip along the north-western banks of Lake Hawea, as the road approaches the narrow strip of land through to Lake Wanaka and beyond, will take your breath away.

Beautiful Lake Hawea was raised some 20 metres (65 feet) in 1958 when its outlet was dammed for the storage of water for the Roxburgh hydro-electric power station. The rising waters drowned the beaches and gentle slope of the shoreline so that the lake has a very different appearance from Lake Wanaka. The colour too is very different, with the depth of water (410 metres/1345 feet) creating a more vivid blue.

Before rising over the Neck, the road drops to lake level, and then follows the shores of

Lake Wanaka where, on a still cloudless day, the mountains can be reflected in almost exact duplicate. Sheer rugged ridges plunge into the lake waters with sunlight and shadows refracting their edges. This is alpine grandeur at its best.

Once Lake Wanaka is left behind, the road runs through an open valley to Makarora, an area which was once densely forested. From the 1860s kahikatea, beech and matai logs were pit-sawn and floated on rafts down Lake Wanaka and the Clutha River to Central Otago.

At Makarora the road enters Mt Aspiring National Park, New Zealand's tenth national park, gazetted on 10 December 1964 and given World Heritage status in December 1990. This treasured alpine area has been opened up to more and more public use since the road through the pass was sealed to provide easy motoring. Walkways, from five-minute ambles to two-hour climbs, can be accessed along the way, leading to aptly named sights such as Blue Pools, Fantail Falls, Thunder Creek Falls and Roaring Billy. At the Gates of Haast gorge, travellers stop to photograph wild water as it crashes over river boulders. At the Blue Pools, rainbow trout appear suspended above the pool floor in the deep crystal-clear waters.

The Haast Pass road follows an ancient trail used by Maori travelling to the West Coast in search of pounamu/greenstone. The name for the trail is Tiora-patea, meaning 'The way is clear'.

The way was not so clear, however, in determining who was the first European to traverse the Alps from Lake Wanaka to the West Coast. Gold prospector Charles

The Gates of Haast

Cameron wanted to reach the West Coast by the most direct route from Dunedin. He crossed the pass alone in January 1863. Just to the west of the pass he buried his powder flask. Close behind him came Julius von Haast whose party of five found the journey very difficult, with constant rain and flooded rivers. Their progress was slow and they ran short of food. Haast named the pass after himself and claimed to be the first European to have travelled through it. Awe of his endeavours and the credibility of his claim were later destroyed, however, by the discovery of Cameron's flask.

Even though Haast Pass is the lowest pass across the Main Divide (563 metres/1847 feet above sea level), the road downwards is extremely steep and slipways have been created at intervals along the road to provide safe exit for vehicles in difficulties. Sheer rock ridges and roaring rivers make this a world of wonder and majesty.

Queenstown facts

- The economy of the Queenstown–Lakes district was founded on sheep farming and grew dramatically when gold was discovered in the 1860s. Now tourism is the driving force, along with farming, stone-fruit and wine. The film industry is developing a strong stake in the local economy too.
- The Queenstown–Lakes district resident population is approximately 18,000.
- The district attracts up to 1.2 million visitors per year. The average day population in 2006 was estimated at 34,000, peaking at 75,000.
- The population of Queenstown is approximately 8500. The population of Arrowtown is around 2400. Wanaka has a permanent population of around 5000 and a transient workforce increases it to about 7000 during the height of winter and summer.
- In its Regional Tourism Forecast data from 2006 to 2013 The Ministry of Tourism expects the number of guest nights spent in Queenstown to increase 22 per cent from 3.36 million to 4.10 million.
- The minimum age for doing a bungy jump at the Kawarau Bridge is 10 years old and the maximum weight is 235 kg (518 pounds).
- The surface of Lake Wakatipu is 309 metres (1014 feet) above sea level. At its deepest point it is 68 metres (223 feet) below sea level.
- Some 80,000 people attended the Warbirds Over Wanaka airshow in 2008.

Queenstown mean daily maximum and minimum temperatures

	Maximum (°C/°F)	Minimum (°C/°F)
Jan	22.5/72.5	10.7/51.3
Feb	22.5/72.5	10.5/50.9
Mar	19.8/67.6	8.8/48.0
Apr	16.1/60.9	6.2/47.8
May	11.7/53.1	3.2/37.8
Jun	8.5/47.3	0.6/33.1
Jul	8.1/46.6	0.1/32.2
Aug	10.3/50.5	1.3/34.3
Sept	13.4/56.1	3.6/38.5
Oct	16.1/60.9	5.5/41.9
Nov	18.8/65.8	7.5/45.5
Dec	20.7/69.2	9.5/49.1
Average	15.7/60.2	5.6/42.1

Mean annual rainfall: 900 mm (35.5 inches)
Mean annual sunshine hours: 1913

(Source: www.metservice.co.nz)